THE IDEOLOGICAL FALLACIES
OF COMMUNISM

STAFF CONSULTATIONS WITH
RABBI S. ANDHIL FINEBERG
BISHOP FULTON J. SHEEN
DR. DANIEL A. POLING

COMMITTEE ON UN-AMERICAN ACTIVITIES
HOUSE OF REPRESENTATIVES
EIGHTY-FIFTH CONGRESS
FIRST SESSION

SEPTEMBER 4, 1957
SEPTEMBER 25, 1957
OCTOBER 18, 1957

(INCLUDING INDEX)

Printed for the use of the Committee on Un-American Activities

UNITED STATES
GOVERNMENT PRINTING OFFICE
22087° WASHINGTON : 1958

COMMITTEE ON UN-AMERICAN ACTIVITIES

UNITED STATES HOUSE OF REPRESENTATIVES

FRANCIS E. WALTER, Pennsylvania, *Chairman*

MORGAN M. MOULDER, Missouri	BERNARD W. KEARNEY, New York
CLYDE DOYLE, California	DONALD L. JACKSON, California
JAMES B. FRAZIER, JR., Tennessee	GORDON H. SCHERER, Ohio
EDWIN E. WILLIS, Louisiana	ROBERT J. McINTOSH, Michigan

RICHARD ARENS, *Director*

H. Res. 458

IN THE HOUSE OF REPRESENTATIVES, U. S.,
February 19, 1958.

Resolved, That there be printed thirty thousand six hundred additional copies of the staff consultations entitled, "The Ideological Fallacies of Communism", held by the Committee on Un-American Activities during the Eighty-fifth Congress, first session, ten thousand six hundred of which shall be for the use of that committee and twenty thousand to be prorated to the Members of the House of Representatives for a period of ninety days, after which time the unused balance shall revert to the Committee on Un-American Activities.

Attest:

RALPH R. ROBERTS, *Clerk.*

II

CONTENTS

The legislation under which the House Committee on Un-American Activities operates is Public Law 601, 79th Congress [1946], chapter 753, 2d session, which provides:

Be it enacted by the Senate and House of Representatives of the United States of America in Congress assembled, * * *

PART 2—RULES OF THE HOUSE OF REPRESENTATIVES

RULE X

SEC. 121. STANDING COMMITTEES

*　　　*　　　*　　　*　　　*　　　*　　　*

17. Committee on Un-American Activities, to consist of nine Members.

RULE XI

POWERS AND DUTIES OF COMMITTEES

*　　　*　　　*　　　*　　　*　　　*　　　*

(q) (1) Committee on Un-American Activities.
(A) Un-American activities.
(2) The Committee on Un-American Activities, as a whole or by subcommittee, is authorized to make from time to time investigations of (i) the extent, character, and objects of un-American propaganda activities in the United States, (ii) the diffusion within the United States of subversive and un-American propaganda that is instigated from foreign countries or of a domestic origin and attacks the principle of the form of government as guaranteed by our Constitution, and (iii) all other questions in relation thereto that would aid Congress in any necessary remedial legislation.

The Committee on Un-American Activities shall report to the House (or to the Clerk of the House if the House is not in session) the results of any such investigation, together with such recommendations as it deems advisable.

For the purpose of any such investigation, the Committee on Un-American Activities, or any subcommittee thereof, is authorized to sit and act at such times and places within the United States, whether or not the House is sitting, has recessed, or has adjourned, to hold such hearings, to require the attendance of such witnesses and the production of such books, papers, and documents, and to take such testimony, as it deems necessary. Subpenas may be issued under the signature of the chairman of the committee or any subcommittee, or by any member designated by any such chairman, and may be served by any person designated by any such chairman or member.

*　　　*　　　*　　　*　　　*　　　*　　　*

RULE XII

LEGISLATIVE OVERSIGHT BY STANDING COMMITTEES

SEC. 136. To assist the Congress in appraising the administration of the laws and in developing such amendments or related legislation as it may deem necessary, each standing committee of the Senate and the House of Representatives shall exercise continuous watchfulness of the execution by the administrative agencies concerned of any laws, the subject matter of which is within the jurisdiction of such committee; and, for that purpose, shall study all pertinent reports and data submitted to the Congress by the agencies in the executive branch of the Government.

RULES ADOPTED BY THE 85TH CONGRESS

House Resolution 5, January 3, 1957

* * * * * * *

RULE X

STANDING COMMITTEES

1. There shall be elected by the House, at the commencement of each Congress,

* * * * * * *

(q) Committee on Un-American Activities, to consist of nine Members.

* * * * * * *

RULE XI

POWERS AND DUTIES OF COMMITTEES

* * * * * * *

17. Committee on Un-American Activities.

(a) Un-American activities.

(b) The Committee on Un-American Activities, as a whole or by subcommittee, is authorized to make from time to time investigations of (1) the extent, character, and objects of un-American propaganda activities in the United States, (2) the diffusion within the United States of subversive and un-American propaganda that is instigated from foreign countries or of a domestic origin and attacks the principle of the form of government as guaranteed by our Constitution, and (3) all other questions in relation thereto that would aid Congress in any necessary remedial legislation.

The Committee on Un-American Activities shall report to the House (or to the Clerk of the House if the House is not in session) the results of any such investigation, together with such recommendations as it deems advisable.

For the purpose of any such investigation, the Committee on Un-American Activities, or any subcommittee thereof, is authorized to sit and act at such times and places within the United States, whether or not the House is sitting, has recessed, or has adjourned, to hold such hearings, to require the attendance of such witnesses and the production of such books, papers, and documents, and to take such testimony, as it deems necessary. Subpenas may be issued under the signature of the chairman of the committee or any subcommittee, or by any member designated by such chairman, and may be served by any person designated by any such chairman or member.

* * * * * * *

26. To assist the House in appraising the administration of the laws and in developing such amendments or related legislation as it may deem necessary, each standing committee of the House shall exercise continuous watchfulness of the execution by the administrative agencies concerned of any laws, the subject matter of which is within the jurisdiction of such committee; and, for that purpose, shall study all pertinent reports and data submitted to the House by the agencies in the executive branch of the Government.

* * * Communism, like crime, advances and takes hold because men ignore God. The real danger in communism lies in the fact that it is atheistic and seeks to replace the Supreme Being. Communism is secularism on the march. It is the mortal foe of all the world's religions which acknowledge the existence of God. Either the faith of our fathers will triumph or communism will engulf us. In this land of ours the two cannot live side by side.

Nowhere among the leaders of the Communist Party in the United States, Russia, Red China or in any other part of the world will you find one who loves and believes in God. God is truth. Communists hate truth and, therefore, they hate the church.

One of the leading slogans of the Communist revolution in Russia in 1917 was: "Religion is the opium of the people."

This was first uttered by Karl Marx, the founder of communism, in 1843. Lenin, now resurrected by the Kremlin as the Communist idol and guide of the present and future, restated it in 1905. And last year, Nikita Khrushchev, the present head of the Russian Communist Party, publicly proclaimed that Communists have not changed their opinion on religion and said:

> We remain the atheists that we have always been;
> we are doing all we can to liberate those people who
> are still under the spell of this religious opiate.

When Communists temporarily and passively tolerate religion, it is for the purpose of furthering communism. But time and again they have struck ruthlessly against Christians, Jews, and other faiths, torturing, imprisoning, and murdering those who hold God above the state. Those who hate God always bring misery in their wake. They are brutal, cruel, and deceitful. Communism denies and destroys every spiritual value. No church and no church member can temporize with it. * * *—J. EDGAR HOOVER, *Director, Federal Bureau of Investigation*.

THE IDEOLOGICAL FALLACIES OF COMMUNISM

SYNOPSIS

Three prominent clergymen—of the Jewish, Catholic, and Protestant faiths, respectively—analyzed in the accompanying staff consultations "The Ideological Fallacies of Communism."

Rabbi S. Andhil Fineberg, community-relations consultant of the American Jewish Committee, characterized communism as follows:

> Communism is a totalitarian scheme for regimenting human existence. It subjects every aspect of life to the wishes and whims of a bureaucratic oligarchy. It is as different from our outlook on life as atheism is different from faith in God. The political and economic aspects of communism are derivatives of a philosophy whose ultimates cannot resemble ours.
>
> Communists base their view of life on materialism and on a collective society. Our way of life is based on Judaeo-Christian concepts and on the importance of even the most humble individual. They think of people as creatures whose destiny is determined solely by their material well-being. We think of people as creatures with souls, who prize spiritual values.

He discussed the ideological fallacies of communism concerning God, man, private property, and power. Regarding the fallacy of communism with respect to the existence of God, Dr. Fineberg stated:

> Ruling out, as they do, the existence of a deity and man's responsibility to that Higher Power, they revere only human beings. They have no hope of the hereafter; they have no concept such as the Jews have—which, incidentally, is the theme of our high holy days—that everyone is accountable to the Divine Judge. They, therefore, do not have what religious people consider higher moral laws, the immutable demands that God makes upon human beings and which are at the base not only of our aspirations but of our concepts of moral conduct.

His comments with reference to the Communist fallacy in regard to man included these observations:

> Lacking a spiritual basis for existence, Communist ideologists conceive of people as having no other worthy objective but material prosperity and military might. All other human ideals, hopes, and aspirations are sacrificed for these. And, in pursuit of these goals for the nation as a whole, Communist rulers assume the right to deal with all human beings as though they were the property and chattel of the state. Democratic leaders would never set up one-party government. You will recall that, when the great emanci-

pator Moses was told that several people were speaking against him in the camp, he welcomed that dissent and said, "Would that all the people were prophets and that God would put His spirit in all of them."

Continuing his analysis, Dr. Fineberg assailed the fallacies of communism in regard to private property by pointing out that—

* * * where property right is so limited that the concept of ownership becomes a myth and a deception, as it is under communism, there ceases to be the kind of personal responsibility necessary for a genuinely religious life, which must be one of owning, of giving, and of sharing, with considerable opportunity for voluntary conduct.

In regard to the fallacy of communism respecting power, Dr. Fineberg exploded the theory of communism "that the beneficence of Communists is sufficient to guarantee good government."

In response to the query as to how the forces of freedom can best combat the ideology of communism, he pointed out that the forces of freedom should emphasize the "proof of the superiority of our way of life over life under communism in terms of religious and spiritual values."

Bishop Fulton J. Sheen, national director of the Society for the Propagation of the Faith, Auxiliary Bishop of New York and Titular Bishop of Cesariana, stated that—

* * * communism is not an economic system; communism is basically a philosophical system, which was born of the marriage of two unmarriageable and unproductive units * * * not based on reality.

He pointed out that—

* * * the existence of God and private property are both denied simultaneously by communism. If a man has no soul, he cannot allege that he has any relationships with anyone outside of the state. If he has no property, he is dependent upon the state even for his physical existence. Therefore the denial of God and the denial of freedom are both conditions of slavery.

He continued:

The goal of communism is the complete subjection of mankind to a totalitarian system which would deny both internal and external freedom.

With reference to the relationship between the philosophy of communism and communism in action, Bishop Sheen observed that—

* * * as in Christianity the word became flesh, or truth became incarnate; in communism the ideology has become action. There is no great diversity between any principles of communism and communism in action. And that is why many people go wrong in judging communism, because they, not knowing its ideology, do not understand the present action.

We of the Western World judge Russia by its foreign policy. Whenever there are smiles at Geneva and Russia apparently begins to be lenient with the Western World, we think communism is good. Whereas if you judge it from its ideology, it is a tactic, but not a change of system.

In regard to the reason for the tremendous inroads made by communism in the course of the last 50 years, Bishop Sheen stated:

There are many reasons for that. One reason is the spiritual vacuum that has been created in the world. The modern world has lost its faith, it has lost its goal and its purpose. And the world became sick and tired of milk-and-water systems where there was nothing so sacred that you could dedicate your life to it, and nothing so evil that you should risk your life to destroy it. And communism comes into a world that is sick with relativism, and offers an absolute, and men find a loyalty and a dedication and a consecration which gives them great faith in a political system, without imposing any individual morality.

As to why certain persons become Communists, Bishop Sheen noted that communism—

* * * legislates for the mass, but it does not impose any individual morality. That is one of the reasons, I think, why some people—not all, God forbid—have an exaggerated interest in social justice, because it dispenses them from individual justice; they begin taking care of everyone else's problems in order to cover up their own dark and rotten conscience. Whenever I hear people talk about social justice I always want to find out how much they pay their housekeepers.

He continued:

It is always well to investigate the moral background of those who become Communists, as it is always a good principle in talking to people not to be so interested in what they say as in why they say it. Why do certain people say certain things? For example, if you ask me a question, and I immediately begin insulting you or the committee, you shouldn't pay any attention to what I am saying, but to why do I say it, to what is wrong with me.

A young man one day knocked Lincoln down in a hospital in Virginia. He didn't recognize Lincoln, and he said to Lincoln, "Why didn't you get out of the way, you big, long-legged spider?" And Lincoln said, "Young man, what's troubling you on the inside?"

Very often skepticism is a moral position; that is to say, it has been determined by behavior. So the intelligentsia will sometimes follow communism because of their behavior.

Among the courses of action which he suggested in undertaking to cope with the international Communist menace was the expulsion of Russia from the United Nations, and the insistence by the West on the liberation of certain suppressed peoples.

Dr. Daniel A. Poling, editor of the Christian Herald, stated that—

Communism is a driving dynamic faith. It has all of the passion that we associate with the early Christian church. But its basic tenet, its first principle, is atheism. It not only disregards, but it refutes and denies, the Christian ethic. It has absolutely no concern for the individual. We believe that government is made for man, and not man for government. Communism teaches and practices that the individual is not only the servant of, but the slave of, the state. He exists for the state. His personal well-being is of no consideration at all if the strength of the state is in any way mitigated or jeopardized by this individual. * * * Communism is a total and comprehensive philosophy. It is a way of life. It is a coverall, body, mind, and soul. It is the universal enslavement.

Dr. Poling pointed out that so-called peaceful coexistence with the Kremlin is both incredible and impossible, that so far as the Kremlin is concerned peaceful coexistence means peaceful submission.

"Communism," Dr. Poling continued, "has made, in the opinion of some of us, a moral debacle of the United Nations." He asserted "that there was every reason for us to withdraw recognition of Russia." He urged that individual citizens join in the efforts of the several patriotic organizations of the Nation which are dedicated to resisting communism.

In regard to the manner in which the forces of freedom can compete in the world market place of ideas with Communist ideology he stated:

* * * We need to emphasize not what material things we have here, but the realities of freedom and the fact that communism is slavery. It is the destruction of the very aspirations of the soul. It is enslavement of the body, and you can prove that by pointing to Communist slave camps all over the world, and not only the enslavement of the body, but the enslavement of the mind and the soul. And remember one thing; there are more than one billion human beings who believe in one God—the Moslem, the Buddhist, the Roman Catholic, the Protestant, and the Jew.

We should lay emphasis upon the fact that communism in its first tenet is atheism. We have obscured that idea too often. We need to point to what we have on our coins, "In God We Trust." We need to get that across, if you please. We are getting the dollar across, but we need to get across the thing that we really finally live by in this country.

THE IDEOLOGICAL FALLACIES OF COMMUNISM

WEDNESDAY, SEPTEMBER 4, 1957

United States House of Representatives,
Committee on Un-American Activities,
Washington, D. C.

STAFF CONSULTATION

The following consultation with Dr. S. Andhil Fineberg was held by the staff of the Committee on Un-American Activities at 10:10 a. m., Wednesday, September 4, 1957, in room 226, Old House Office Building, Washington, D. C.

Staff members present: Richard Arens, director (presiding); Richard S. Weil, staff member; and Col. William F. Heimlich, consultant.

Mr. Arens. Today we shall consider "The Ideological Fallacies of Communism."

We are pleased to welcome to the consultation on this subject Rabbi S. Andhil Fineberg, who is the community-relations consultant of the American Jewish Committee.

RABBI S. ANDHIL FINEBERG

Mr. Arens. We would like, for the purpose of this record, if you please, sir, your name residence, and occupation.

Dr. Fineberg. My name is S. Andhil Fineberg. I reside in Mount Vernon, N. Y. I received my doctorate from Columbia University. I have occupied pulpits in Niagara Falls, N. Y.; Pittsburgh, Pa.; and Mount Vernon, N. Y.

Mr. Arens. Please give us a word about how you first became interested in the subject of communism.

Dr. Fineberg. For the past 10 years I have directed the program against communism of the American Jewish Committee, but my interest in the subject began when I was serving in the United States Marine Corps during World War 1. Among my friends were Mr. and Mrs. Boris Bogen, of Cincinnati, who were thoroughly acquainted with Russian political developments. When the Czar was deposed in March 1917, they were very happy.

They were horrified when the Bolsheviks, an insignificant part of the Russian population, violently came to power in October of the same year. The Bogens knew that the Bolsheviks, or the Communists as they were later called, were totalitarians who destroyed a democratic Russian government. I learned the facts in 1918 from people who knew that these new rulers of Russia were militant atheists steeped in theories of economic determinism and dedicated to the proposition that human beings do not possess souls, nor conscience, nor obligations to Deity.

Mr. Arens. May I ask, Dr. Fineberg, whether you would characterize communism as just another economic or political system?

1

Dr. FINEBERG. If the communism of the Soviet Union involved only a difference of political theories, or of economic theories, as some Americans have fatuously believed, we could debate the merits of communism in this country dispassionately.

Mr. ARENS. What, then, is communism?

Dr. FINEBERG. Communism is a totalitarian scheme for regimenting human existence. It subjects every aspect of life to the wishes and whims of a bureaucratic oligarchy. It is as different from our outlook on life as atheism is different from faith in God. The political and economic aspects of communism are derivatives of a philosophy whose ultimates cannot resemble ours.

Communists base their view of life on materialism and on a collective society. Our way of life is based on Judaeo-Christian concepts and on the importance of even the most humble individual. They think of people as creatures whose destiny is determined solely by their material well-being. We think of people as creatures with souls, who prize spiritual values.

Mr. ARENS. Dr. Fineberg, you are a man of the cloth of a great religious faith. Please tell us if there is a basis for coexistence or consistency between adherents of the Jewish faith and adherents of communism.

Dr. FINEBERG. As far as coexistence is concerned, religious people have always accepted the idea that we must be willing, while opposing evil, to live with it. I reject the thought that there must be inevitable military war with the Communists, a clash which would end in vast destruction, but I wish to say, unequivocally, that Judaism and communism are absolutely incompatible. As early as 1919, the American Jewish Committee declared:

Everything that bolshevism stands for is, to the Jew, detestable. The Jewish traditions wed him to law and order. The Bolshevists are the enemies of law and order. * * * The great mass of the Jews are faithful to their ancient religion, and are ever ready to help their brethren in distress. The club of the Bolshevist knows no brother and he despises religion.

Mr. ARENS. Have the religious forces of the world, in your judgment, been as vigorous in opposition to the spread of communism as they might have been?

Dr. FINEBERG. Too few religious leaders have accepted the responsibility of refuting Communist propaganda. Like most Americans, clergymen have been against communism without studying it and without effort to expose its fallacies.

Mr. ARENS. How do you account for that?

Dr. FINEBERG. Most religious leaders have taken the view that the best way to combat communism is to perfect our own Nation. "Let us be thoroughly honest," they say, in effect, "and no one will cheat us. Let us not attack communism lest we injure civil liberties in our own land."

In the main I agree with the proposition that the first obligation of religious people is to set our own house in order and to improve our own system. But I believe it is an error to stop there. One cannot keep thieves from breaking into our houses by merely being honest, and I have never seen an instance where counterfeit coin was banished by merely minting more good money.

Mr. ARENS. Would you draw a distinction between the activities of the Communists and the ideology of communism?

Dr. FINEBERG. The villainies of Communist leaders have become well known. But unfortunately people assume that these scoundrels acted contrary to Communist doctrines. Even Stalin, having been denounced by Communists, is assumed to have acted in an anti-Communist fashion. Actually, Stalin and all the other Communist bureaucrats whose villainies are now known were and are the incarnation of communism. They were thoroughly indoctrinated and whole-hearted Communists. They did what communism required of them, even though their comrades later made scapegoats of them.

Political murder and kidnaping, ruthless purges that slaughter multitudes, imprisonment and execution without trial, and other such atrocities have been customary under communism because that is what communism brings. No government, including our own, can guarantee that everyone will respect the civil rights and civil liberties of others. But enormous injustices are inherent and inescapable under communism. They are inevitable where power is so highly centralized. We cannot point out often enough that it is Communist ideology which is responsible for the countless crimes of Communist bureaucrats.

Mr. ARENS. Dr. Fineberg, what do you consider to be the principal ideological fallacies of communism, which cause the reprehensible Communist conduct, to which you have alluded?

Dr. FINEBERG. Those fallacies are concerning God, man, private property, and power, to mention only the principal ones.

Mr. ARENS. Then may we proceed, if you please, with consideration of each of these principal elements. First of all, what is the fallacy of communism with respect to the existence of a supreme deity, God?

Dr. FINEBERG. Ruling out, as they do, the existence of a deity and man's responsibility to that Higher Power, they revere only human beings. They have no hope of the hereafter; they have no concept such as the Jews have, which, incidentally, is the theme of our High Holy Days, that everyone is accountable to the Divine Judge. They, therefore, do not have what religious people consider higher moral laws, the immutable demands that God makes upon human beings and which are at the base not only of our aspirations but of our concepts of moral conduct.

In Judaism, we say, "Put not your trust in princes." We believe that without divine inspiration and that which the Creator gives us of his own eternal wisdom, we would flounder forever from one temptation to another. In brief, unless the Creator has provided for man's morality, human life must resemble jungle life.

Mr. WEIL. Would you say ours is a religious nation?

Dr. FINEBERG. In our society there are many agnostics and some atheists, but there is tremendous respect for religion and for those values which can be readily traced to religious authority. Americans are guaranteed genuine religious liberty. Behind the Iron Curtain religion has been drastically curtailed and atheism has been state promoted.

Mr. ARENS. Now, having dealt with Communist negation of the concept of God and of all religion, may I invite your attention to the second fallacy which you suggest in the ideology of communism, namely, Communist fallacy with reference to man.

Dr. FINEBERG. Lacking a spiritual basis for existence, Communist ideologists conceive of people as having no other worthy objective but material prosperity and military might. All other human ideals, hopes, and aspirations are sacrificed for these. And in pursuit of these goals for the nation as a whole, Communist rulers assume the right to deal with all human beings as though they were the property and chattel of the state. Democratic leaders would never set up one-party government. You will recall that when the great emancipator Moses was told that several people were speaking against him in the camp, he welcomed that dissent and said, "Would that all the people were prophets and that God would put His spirit in all of them."

The Communists claim that someday there will be, as a result of their efforts, a humanity which will somehow maintain an earthly paradise with no government at all. Toward the promised "wither-ing away" of the governments they have established, the Communists have made no progress whatsoever. Far from bringing about a classless society where all people are equal, the Communists way of life has widened the gap between those who possess power and those who lack it. What Communism does to people has been well de-scribed in Milovan Djilas' book, The New Class. Communists form an elite master group while the overwhelming majority of the popula-tion are deprived of the most essential features of desirable existence, such as the power to make important decisions, the right to engage in political action, and the opportunity for effective dissent. This is why I say communism is a way of life entirely different from our own.

There is no escape in a Communist regime from Lenin's democratic centralism, incidentally, another example of the depravity of Com-munist language. Democratic centralism compels everyone to yield resignedly to the decisions that those at the top make. No one is permitted to question the rightfulness of those decisions. Anyone who can call that democratic when it applies, as it does in Communist-controlled countries, to every facet of existence, is already in intellec-tual bondage.

Mr. ARENS. Now, may we consider the third fallacy which you suggest in the ideology of communism, namely, its concept with reference to private property.

Dr. FINEBERG. Neither Judaism nor Christianity has challenged the right of private property. The Bible assumes, as does nearly all of our religious literature, that every individual should have some material possessions. However, according to the religious view of things, no one possesses anything without obligation and responsi-bility to others. Religious people assume that they must use what-ever property they have not only for their own benefit, but also for the welfare of others.

Let me say parenthetically that there has been no objection in re-ligious thinking to people who agree to common ownership such as a partnership or a corporation or a cooperative. There is no religious objection to a nation's running its post office or owning its railroads. But where property right is so limited that the concept of ownership becomes a myth and a deception, as it is under communism, there ceases to be the kind of personal responsibility necessary for a genu-inely religious life, which must be one of owning, of giving, and of sharing, with considerable opportunity for voluntary conduct. The good life, as we envision and experience it, is impossible without some personal independence.

Let me explain this by comparing the status of a man who serves as the captain of a ship owned by a private corporation. How ridiculous it would be if he resigned his office and became a sailor on a United States Navy boat, saying, "Now I own my own ship." The fact that all citizens of the United States "own" the Navy does not create any such situation as the word "ownership" describes when a man owns his own boat. In fact, a government employee is independent only in a country where private employment is open to him. It is in a free market with private enterprise that one can enjoy greatest independence and freedom of action. It would be better to have a dozen Scrooges competing for one's labor or competing for one's produce than to have one monopolistic government as the sole employer and purchaser. Total government ownership destroys the possibility of freedom of thought and action.

Property is so closely related to the individual's choice of conduct and to his way of life that Judaism has always recognized private property rights. Jews developed many laws regulating inheritance and transfer of property, business activities, and the like, but private property was never declared to be an evil per se, as it is under communism. Under communism the individual loses along with his property, his opportunity of expression in the arts, and for the development of his culture. Let me cite the fact that there is no law in Russia against printing a Hebrew book, but for 40 years none was printed because no one could get the paper or type. In a free society every cultural group can publish what it pleases. In a Communist country, a culture must die if the hierarchy refuses to let it have the physical means of producing books and periodicals.

A cruel fallacy of communism is the impression created among innumerable people that ownership is identical when the individual owns something and when "society" owns it. In actuality, there is a vast difference in ownerships. Individuals and small groups manage and control that which they own, while the "possessions" of 50 or 100 million people must be managed and controlled by the relatively few at the top. In America, the electorate can at least change the administrators by ballot. In a Communist country, none but the top administrators can make any important change of any kind.

Mr. Arens. And now, if you please, what about the fourth fallacy which you have suggested in the ideology of communism, namely, its concept of power?

Dr. Fineberg. Among democratic people, there is a great distrust of government. We hedge the power of those who control government by a great many devices. I need hardly tell Americans of the many limits that restrict and restrain those who govern us. We keep the man who obtains political power from thereby acquiring power over our press, over our educational institutions, and over our various cultural and social activities. We encourage a tremendous number of voluntary organizations to do things which the government might do. But the primary point I want to make here is that there is a skepticism about those who govern. No man is considered so righteous that power may not corrupt him.

Among Communists, on the other hand, the theory is that the beneficence of Communists is sufficient to guarantee good government. They excoriate people of wealth and those whom they call "the ruling classes" in non-Communist countries and say: "We perfectly wonderful benevolent unselfish creatures will take over all of the power that the Fascists have but we must have a great deal more power—unlimited power. We will assume the reins of government and being determined as we are to advance the good of everyone, we will create that heaven which does not exist even in the hereafter." Amazingly, many people put such faith in human beings as a Communist despotism requires of its followers.

Mr. ARENS. Is that why the Communist doctrine has had such fantastic success in sweeping vast areas of the world in so short a time?

Dr. FINEBERG. That is part of the reason. Where people are so unhappy that they crave drastic social change, they are likely to accept glittering promises such as the Communists make. Unless analyzed and disproved, Communist theories are highly alluring. But it would be a grave error to think that Communists, with all of their wretched failures and unpardonable brutalities can point to no successes. To be sure they deceive, beguile, and betray, but they can boast of some triumphs in rapid industrialization.

Mr. ARENS. Now may I invite your attention to an area of inquiry that should be of immediate practical concern to all of us, namely, how can the forces of freedom best combat in the world market place the ideology of communism?

Dr. FINEBERG. I am glad you limited your question to the matter of ideology because there are many things our Nation has to do abroad to meet the threat of communism, such as foreign aid, military assistance, exchange programs, technical assistance programs, and the like; but in regard to ideology I would say that we must begin at home right here in the United States. We must overcome the idea that communism will doom or destroy itself. We must cease to let this be a one-sided intellectual war, with the Communists using every facility while many of our best minds are apathetic.

In Communist schools the relative merits of communism and of Western Democracy are constantly contrasted. The faults and deficiencies that crop up in Western culture are magnified. The virtues are overlooked. But this process has been going on continually and it has produced extremely capable propagandists for the Communists. When courses of study or even lectures concerning communism are suggested in the United States, someone always is on the spot to declare that such instruction is altogether unnecessary.

As long as the American public refuses to examine the theories of communism and to understand the fallacies, this tremendous movement which has declared from its inception that it will destroy the religious way of life and expunge our American outlook on life, is bound to win many a contest for the minds of men.

Mr. ARENS. Can we win this struggle for the minds of men by an approach which tells of the productivity of this Nation, how we can produce more television sets and automobiles and things of material value than can the Communist society; or should our approach, in your judgment, point out the ideological, spiritual fallacies of communism and how communism has an ideology which is diametrically opposed to the undergirding forces of our free society?

Dr. FINEBERG. You have put your finger on one of the fallacies underlying our own efforts to combat communism which we would not have made had our clergy, our educators, and others of our best minds not run away from this subject.

If all that people want is more food, better machinery, and bigger guns, the Communists will have as much to offer as we have, as far as national product is concerned. What use will be made of it is another matter. Communist planners are capable materialists, ready to sacrifice all other considerations. They are not deflected by spiritual or religious considerations. Because of their bureaucratic system and their failure to take the human soul into account, they have some bad economic problems; but they can solve those by doing as they have heretofore, by herding millions of people into slave-labor camps and by exacting every last bit of labor and sacrifice from the toiling masses.

When we tell people in backward countries of our many bathtubs and our splendid cars, the Russian propagandist had better be taken into account, for he says "the reason the imperialists have all these luxuries is that they took your oil, your rubber, and your other raw materials."

If all that we can do is offer material advancement, let us not forget that the Communist countries offer the same things. It is foolhardy to say that all you need do is to give people a better material existence to keep them out of communism at the very time that the Soviet Union itself is willing to help backward countries materially.

What Communists cannot offer, what they do not have, and what we can provide is best described as "spiritual values." We can supply, if our clergy will furnish the material, proof of the superiority of our way of life over life under communism in terms of religious and spiritual values.

Mr. ARENS. We thank you, Dr. Fineberg, for your contribution to the subject, "The Ideological Fallacies of Communism."

Dr. FINEBERG. Let me say it has been a pleasure to be here discussing this subject with you. I hope that the House Committee on Un-American Activities will continue its efforts to educate the American public on the nature of communism. It should be apparent that exposing the misdeeds of Communists is not enough. We must not fail to expose the soulless nature of communism and to refute the deceptive arguments of its ideologists. In the tremendous battle for the minds of men religious leaders everywhere should see to it that something more than the needs of the body are brought into account.

(Thereupon, at 12:35 p. m., Wednesday, September 4, 1957, the staff consultation was concluded.)

THE IDEOLOGICAL FALLACIES OF COMMUNISM

WEDNESDAY, SEPTEMBER 25, 1957

UNITED STATES HOUSE OF REPRESENTATIVES,
COMMITTEE ON UN-AMERICAN ACTIVITIES,
New York, N. Y.

STAFF CONSULTATION

The following consultation with Bishop Fulton J. Sheen of the Catholic Church, was held by the staff of the Committee on Un-American Activities, at the offices of the Society for the Propagation of the Faith, 366 Fifth Avenue, New York, N. Y., at 3 p. m., on Wednesday, September 25, 1957.

Staff members present: Richard Arens, director (presiding), and Col. William F. Heimlich, consultant.

Mr. ARENS. We are pleased at this time, on behalf of the Committee on Un-American Activities of the House of Representatives, to consult with Bishop Fulton J. Sheen, Auxiliary Bishop of New York and Titular Bishop of Cesariana on the subject, "The Ideological Fallacies of Communism."

BISHOP FULTON J. SHEEN

Mr. ARENS. As a point of departure in our consultation, may I ask, Bishop Sheen, if you could give us the benefit of your judgment on the principal ideological fallacies of Communism?

Bishop SHEEN. When one speaks of the ideology of communism one is speaking of a philosophy. That is what it means, basically, ideology.

Well, the first ideological fallacy of communism is that it is an artificial system imposed on reality, both economic and political. What is this artificial system? This artificial system is the conglomeration of two distinct philosophies that were united in the brain of Karl Marx. One was the system of idealism which issued from Hegel, which he was obliged to study, as were all students in Germany. Hegel's philosophy was called dialectical idealism. It was idealism because it was concerned with ideas. It was called dialectical because it was concerned with how ideas developed, mainly by contradiction.

Suppose, for example, we were decorating a room. One said, "Let us decorate it in red," another said, "In green," and we compromise for blue. That would be a development of an idea through contrast, fiction, and contradiction.

After Marx studied this particular system he then read a book of Feuerbach, Ludwig Feuerbach, entitled "The Essence of Christianity," which was an attack upon all Hegelianism and was an affirmation of the crudest kind of materialism.

9

Marx said he was absolutely incapable of controlling his enthusiasm when he read this book, with its emphasis on materialism. Then there came to the brain of Marx the idea of uniting a part of Hegel with Feuerbach. He said, "Wouldn't it be a wonderful idea to take the dialectics which belong to Hegel's idealism and apply them to the materialism of Feuerbach?" If one did that, one would then have dialectical materialism. The philosophy would then be how materialism grows.

Marx then proceeded to show that materialism grows, or everything material grows, by contradiction, the same as Hegel said ideas grow by contradiction. And the example that his colleague Engels gave was that you drop barley on the earth; the barley is negated by the earth; out of the negation of the barley by the earth there comes an entirely new harvest of barley, different in quantity and quality from that which was sowed.

Up to this point it is only a philosophy, but it is a philosophy which is purely mental and without any basis in reality.

He now goes to France, where he meets Proudhon, explains the system to Proudhon, and Proudhon says, "Marx, you are a typical German: this is up in the air; it's too idealistic and nobody will be interested in it." Proudhon suggested that he apply it to the social order.

And the application to the social order was this: Now it is not only matter that has within itself a tension; it is society that has the tension. It is not just barley and earth negating one another; those who own property are negated by those who do not own property, and those who do not own are negated by those who do own; and out of the two comes a new social order, and that new social order is communism.

The point, therefore, is that communism is not an economic system; communism is basically a philosophical system, which was born of the marriage of two unmarriageable and unproductive units; namely, Hegel and Feuerbach.

Mr. ARENS. May I inquire at this point: How does this philosophy of communism compare with reality?

Bishop SHEEN. Well, the first point I made was that it was an ideology that was not based on reality.

Mr. ARENS. I should like at this point, if you please, to ask you to pursue that specific train of thought to tell us how in your judgment, communism varies from or contradicts reality?

Bishop SHEEN. Well, first of all, it is perhaps going into it too philosophically to say that what Marx was really talking about were contraries instead of contradictions, that the earth is not the contradiction of the barley seed, it is something that complements it.

But now getting more precisely down to earth, why is the ideology in conflict with reality? Because it is in conflict even with the reality of communism. Why, if contradiction, dialectics, tension are inherent in nature and in history, why is it that dialectics do not apply to communism? Why doesn't communism beget its negation?

And they have never been able to answer that particular question; the only concrete answer that was ever given to it was Mao Tse-tung's, a month ago, when he said, "You must allow for variations and even new contradictions within a Communist society." And for that Mao Tse-tung has been reproved by the Communists.

Mr. ARENS. Does the philosophy of Communism encompass a concept of God?

Bishop SHEEN. No; there are several reasons why there is no place for God in communism. One is because of its concept of freedom. Suppose I correlate the problem of religion and the problem of freedom in answering your question, and let me begin with freedom and then go to religion.

A man is free on the inside because he has a soul that he can call his own. Wherever you have the spirit you have freedom. A pencil has no freedom, ice has no freedom to be warm, fire has no freedom to be cold. You begin to have freedom only when you have something immaterial or spiritual.

Now, freedom must have some external guaranty of itself. The external guaranty of human freedom is property. A man is free on the inside because he can call his soul his own; he is free on the outside because he can call something he has his own. Therefore private property is the economic guaranty of human freedom.

Suppose now you concoct a system in which you want to possess man totally. On what conditions can you erect a totalitarian system so that man belongs to you completely? One, you have got to deny spirit; two, you have got to deny property.

That is why the existence of God and private property are both denied simultaneously by communism. If a man has no soul, he cannot allege that he has any relationships with anyone outside of the state. If he has no property, he is dependent upon the state even for his physical existence. Therefore the denial of God and the denial of freedom are both conditions of slavery.

Mr. ARENS. Is there, in your judgment, room within the philosophy of communism for moral concepts?

Bishop SHEEN. Yes, there is, if you use moral in the Communist sense of what is expedient or nonexpedient for a totalitarian system. What is true and what is false, what is right, and what is wrong in communism? Anything that favors the Communist cause is right. Anything that deters it or obstructs it is wrong.

What is true under the Communist system? Truth is what is helpful for establishing the revolution; false is what obstructs it.

Mr. ARENS. And what is the goal of communism?

Bishop SHEEN. The goal of communism is the complete subjection of mankind to a totalitarian system which would deny both internal and external freedom.

Mr. ARENS. May I ask you if you see a distinction between the ideology of communism and communism in action; does it work out the way it was conceived to work?

Bishop SHEEN. May I before I answer that question bring out one other point about the ideology——

Mr. ARENS. Please do.

Bishop SHEEN. That will help us, I think, answer that question. It has to do with the problem of what is a person. There is a difference between a person and an individual. An individual is replaceable. When you buy oranges you can say, "I don't like that one, give me this one." But you cannot say that about children.

Every person in the world is irreplaceable and unique. Now, democracy is based upon the concept of persons, not individuals. The political philosophers of communism said that it was based upon individuals, and individuals could be massed, and out of the mass came communism.

Karl Marx discussed the problem of person. He said a person in a democracy is supposed to have value because he has a soul and was created by God. He was perfectly right in saying that that was the basic principle of democracy, but then he went on, in some works that are not very well known, and he reiterated the idea in one of his introductions to "Das Kapital," in which he said the person has value only inasmuch as he is useful to the revolutionary movement. The moment he ceases to be useful, he no longer exists.

That is why liquidation can be right, because right is not in objectivity, right is in what the party determines to be right.

Mr. ARENS. Does not the Communist philosophy have an end result which they perceive to be good, a kind of a millenium on earth?

Bishop SHEEN. Yes; communism has actually taken from Christianity.

Mr. ARENS. It is a perversion of Christianity, however, is it not?

Bishop SHEEN. Oh, yes; certainly. But it has taken from Christianity the notion of a final retribution and judgment; there is no such thing as coming into the Kingdom of God without a trial; individually there is not, collectively the world itself will not pass into another world without a last judgment and a great conflagration.

Now, communism is much more right than the liberalism of the 19th century. The liberalism of the 19th century believed in automatic progress; nothing can stop it. Their view of progress was quite wrong, because all you have to do is simply to count up the interval between wars; the interval between the Franco-Prussian War and the First World War was 45 years; and then between the First World War and the Second, 23, so they are becoming more frequent. Progress is not automatic.

Communism, however, instead of believing in automatic progress, said there has to come a moment of trial, of conflict, of purgation—a kind of a last judgment. That is the moment of violence and revolution, and the imposition of party authority on the mass that is seized. Then there comes peace.

So they have taken over something there from Christianity and perverted it, and they believe in a millennium, but they believed it would happen much more quickly than it has.

Marx, for example, was sure that the last country in the world that would ever be Communist would be Russia, because it did not have the intrinsic contradictions of capital and labor, therefore it could not become communistic. But both Marx and Lenin expected that within 20 or 30 years it would, and the revolutionists of 1917 thought it would be within 5 or 10 years. And the millennium today is receding.

Colonel HEIMLICH. How do you account for the fact that so few people have acquired domination over so many in a state such as Russia, where even Lenin thought such revolution or communism would be impossible?

Bishop SHEEN. It is easy to make a touchdown when you run on the foul lines. Remember that the Communists operate in a much broader field than the rest of the world, who are governed by a very definite sense of right and wrong and respect for human personality and human truth. When you do not obligate yourself to a concept of truth and right, you have a much larger area in which to operate.

Mr. ARENS. Do you perceive a distinction between the philosophy of communism, what communism purports to be, and what communism is in reality as it has been sweeping over approximately one-third of the globe?

Bishop SHEEN. No; I find that, as in Christianity the word became flesh, or truth became incarnate; in communism the ideology has become action. There is no great diversity between any principles of communism and communism in action. And that is why many people go wrong in judging communism, because they, not knowing its ideology, do not understand the present action.

We of the Western World judge Russia by its foreign policy. Whenever there are smiles at Geneva and Russia apparently begins to be lenient with the Western World, we think communism is good. Whereas if you judge it from its ideology, it is a tactic, but not a change of system.

Mr. ARENS. Is there a basis for trust or confidence upon which we could have sound negotiations with the men of the Kremlin?

Bishop SHEEN. There is absolutely no basis. As Lenin himself said, lies, deceit must be used in order to attain the Communist goal.

Mr. ARENS. May I revert, if you please, to the theme that was posed a moment ago, by Colonel Heimlich, namely, in view of the fallacies of communism, why is it communism in the course of the last 50 years has made such tremendous inroads throughout the world?

Bishop SHEEN. There are many reasons for that. One reason is the spiritual vacuum that has been created in the world. The modern world has lost its faith, it has lost its goal and its purpose. And the world became sick and tired of milk-and-water systems where there was nothing so sacred that you could dedicate your life to it, and nothing so evil that you should risk your life to destroy it. And communism comes into a world that is sick with relativism, and offers an absolute, and men find a loyalty and a dedication and a consecration which gives them great faith in a political system, without imposing any individual morality.

Mr. ARENS. You have given us a diagnosis of the disease; do you have a remedy to suggest?

Bishop SHEEN. Remedies can be political, economic, moral, educational. As regards education, I believe in informing people about the philosophy of communism. I insist on the philosophy, because that is the only way that communism will ever be understood.

Politically and juridically, there should be a tightening of our laws so that we could get back to a condition that we had in the days when our country began, when we knew practically only one traitor, and we could name him. And history carried on the name of Benedict Arnold.

Now the name is legion. It is no longer a scandal to the American people that there is a traitor, or that we have traitors by the thousands, perhaps hundreds of thousands.

Colonel HEIMLICH. Does that not indicate, sir, what you said earlier, that this very lack of some spiritual value, some rock on which we can anchor our moral life, is lacking?

Bishop SHEEN. Yes.

Colonel HEIMLICH. And the Communist, as you said—and I thought it was so very well put—has his faith in his system which imposes no morality, a discipline which does not discipline morally.

Bishop SHEEN. It legislates for the mass, but it does not impose any individual morality. That is one of the reasons, I think, why some people—not all, God forbid—have an exaggerated interest in social justice, because it dispenses them from individual justice; they begin taking care of everyone else's problems in order to cover up their own dark and rotten conscience. Whenever I hear people talk about social justice I always want to find out how much they pay their housekeepers.

Mr. ARENS. May I inquire if you feel that is one reason why, in our work in the Committee on Un-American Activities, we find within the Communist network, and within the framework of those who are under Communist discipline, vast segments of the intelligentsia of this country, because they have lost a moral foundation for their lives?

Bishop SHEEN. Yes. It is always well to investigate the moral background of those who become Communists, as it is always a good principle in talking to people not to be so interested in what they say, as in why they say it. Why do certain people say certain things? For example, if you ask me a question, and I immediately begin insulting you or the committee, you shouldn't pay any attention to what I am saying, but to why do I say it, to what is wrong with me.

A young man one day knocked Lincoln down in a hospital in Virginia. He didn't recognize Lincoln, and he said to Lincoln, "Why didn't you get out of the way, you big, long-legged spider?" And Lincoln said, "Young man, what's troubling you on the inside?"

Very often skepticism is a moral position, that is to say, it has been determined by behavior. So the intelligentsia will sometimes follow communism because of their behavior.

Colonel HEIMLICH. What can we as Christians, or as believers in God and God's law and God's creation, do to blunt the attack of this ideology of communism?

Bishop SHEEN. Well, I was going to come to the Christian solution of it in answer to your question, because I mentioned several ways of suggesting remedies.

Mr. ARENS. Proceed, then please, at your own pace.

Bishop SHEEN. I think that the United Nations should expel Russia for certain actions, particularly in Hungary. Two, I think that the United Nations should be turned upside down. You see, the United Nations is made up—and because I haven't thought about this for some time and my language may need some correction—of the Security Council, and then there is the aggregate General Assembly. I think that the General Assembly should be on top, because the General Assembly for the most part is made up of small nations. The small nations must depend upon moral right, since they cannot depend upon physical power. Let them therefore be the legislative, judicial body, and let the Security Council of the powerful nations execute the decisions of the small powers.

And furthermore, when the United Nations was set up it was set up with five powers. Suppose it were set up with 5 policemen who were supposed to take care of the civic peace of New York City, and 1 of the policemen robbed a bank; should he have the right of veto against the other 4 policemen who wanted to arrest him?

Colonel HEIMLICH. Of course this right was insisted on by the Soviet Union, represented by Mr. Molotov, at the time of the San Francisco Conference.

Bishop SHEEN. I know it was, and I talked about it to 25,000 people the night before the United Nations opened in San Francisco; and a New York newspaper carried an editorial making fun of me because I said Russia would abuse the right of veto.

Then as in regard to what Christians can do, remember that Christians are asked to do something for which they have no implementation. We happen to live, remember, in a dualistic civilization. It used to be a unitary civilization, when Christianity was Christendom, and Christendom was civilization. The power and the force of Christianity do not have any organs by which their spiritual and moral power can find action, corrective action. Christianity must operate solely in the realm of suggesting ideas.

Mr. ARENS. I do not quite understand your observation that Christian organizations, churches, and the like, do not have organs by which they can make their ideology effective.

Bishop SHEEN. Well, for example, there is no way of influencing a whole judicial system from a Christian point of view, from a moral point of view, to include Protestants and Jews and Catholics. There is no way for the spiritual forces of the Nation, for example, to influence an economic system or the international order.

Mr. ARENS. Can't they influence them because of their impact upon the individuals who represent the people in the governments?

Bishop SHEEN. Again, that gets back to what I was saying, which was merely the proposing of ideals. The impact is not as it is, for example, in a baseball club, where a man who breaks training can be penalized immediately, or where I myself could be subject to discipline if I refused to obey the laws of the church. It is over them as in our present structure of society the sun is over us, but we can do many things under that sun.

One way in which the spiritual and moral forces of the Nation might be harnessed would be to insist in the United Nations over and over again on the liberation of certain suppressed peoples, particularly Poland. World War II started on account of Poland. Whatever happens to Poland, therefore, will happen to the world. And we should never let go of the question of when is Poland going to decide its own fate, when is Hungary going to, when is Albania, and not be deterred by any other problems. No problem is settled until Poland, Hungary, and the other nations behind the Iron Curtain have their problems settled.

Mr. ARENS. What can the individual do? Here are Mr. and Mrs. Jones out in Dubuque, Iowa, or Kansas City, Mo., or here in New York City; what can they, as just ordinary Americans, do, if anything?

Bishop SHEEN. They can become more articulate about what they believe to be right and good for the world. It happens that we live in a mass civilization. We read the same newspapers; we listen to the same news commentators; we read almost the same magazines; and we settle down to the complacency of mass opinion. And persons to their neighbors will express moral opinions concerning the United Nations, the suppressed peoples behind the Iron and Bamboo Curtains, which they never have expressed to governments and to the United Nations. And if these common people ever express somewhere else than over a back fence their moral convictions concerning what is happening in the world, I think they would make an impact.

Mr. ARENS. Is there some other point that you, of your own volition, would like to make, even though we may not have asked you about it?

Bishop SHEEN. From a purely spiritual point of view, we have been, of course, very much concerned with Russia, since what we call the revelation of Fatima in 1917; from April 13 to October 13, 1917, there were a series of revelations in Fatima about Russia spreading revolution throughout the world. In 1917 we entered the World War. The Kerensky government was falling, or had fallen; the Czar was killed, and no one ever would have thought that Russia would then be a world power.

The fullness of this revelation has never been given out by the church. Some say it will be given out completely in 1960.

The revelation further said that Russia would eventually receive the gift of faith. I think we will live to see, all of us will live to see, the end of communism in Russia. Communism has no way of propagating its masters. The monarchy has; democracy has; communism has none, except exile, cutting throats. Good is self-preserving; evil is always self-defeating.

There is no such thing as the liberation of China until Russia itself disintegrates. I believe that, when Russia does disintegrate, Russia will be one of the great spiritual and moral nations of the world, because one thing that communism has done in Russia is that it has restored a sense of discipline and dedication, which is very much on the decline in the Western World. From a truly Christian point of view, what has happened in Christianity in the modern world is that Christ and His cross have been separated, and the Western World has, to some extent, taken Christ without His cross, and made Him a feminine Kiwanis booster.

Communism has taken the cross without Christ, and when you take the cross without Christ, you get tyranny and concentration camps. There is no love on it; it is a cruel instrument of contradiction. That is the religious situation of the world.

Who is closer to the ultimate reconciliation, of the two? Not the Western World, with its tawdry, cheap, sentimental Christ. Russia is closer, with its cross. And Russia will eventually be one of the greatest spiritual and moral forces in the world, within 50 or 100 years.

Colonel HEIMLICH. When it has restored Christ to its particular cross?

Bishop SHEEN. That's right.

Mr. ARENS. May we conclude the consultation by expressing our thanks for the contribution which you have made to our study of "The Ideological Fallacies of Communism."

(Whereupon, at 3:45 p. m., Wednesday, September 25, 1957, the staff consultation was concluded.)

THE IDEOLOGICAL FALLACIES OF COMMUNISM

FRIDAY, OCTOBER 18, 1957

United States House of Representatives,
Committee on Un-American Activities.
New York, N. Y.

STAFF CONSULTATION

The following consultation with Dr. Daniel A. Poling was held by the staff of the Committee on Un-American Activities at the office of the Christian Herald, 27 East 39th Street, New York City, at 2:30 p. m. on Friday, October 18, 1957.

Staff members present: Richard Arens, director (presiding), and Col. William F. Heimlich, consultant.

Mr. ARENS. We are pleased at this time on behalf of the Committee on Un-American Activities of the House of Representatives to consult with Dr. Daniel A. Poling, the editor of the Christian Herald, with respect to the subject, "The Ideological Fallacies of Communism."

DR. DANIEL A. POLING

Mr. ARENS. Doctor, what do you regard as the principal fallacies in the ideology of communism?

Dr. POLING. Well, sir, communism is a driving dynamic faith. It has all of the passion that we associate with the early Christian church. But its basic tenet, its first principle, is atheism. It not only disregards, but it refutes and denies, the Christian ethic. It has absolutely no concern for the individual. We believe that government is made for man, and not man for government. Communism teaches and practices that the individual is not only the servant of, but the slave of, the state. He exists for the state. His personal well-being is of no consideration at all if the strength of the state is in any way mitigated or jeopardized by this individual.

Communism, as we regard faith and the Christian ethic, is unmoral. This is at the heart of the great and irreconcilable controversy.

Mr. ARENS. Does this faith of communism, or this force of communism, translate itself into action which can be appraised?

Dr. POLING. It does. It translates itself into action. For instance, I have just come back from the Far East. I met an old friend out there who, when I first knew him, was the treasurer of one of our orphanages in Canton. He was a fine young man. He was happy to remain in Canton after the Communists came in because he wished to continue to serve the little children in that orphanage. He was betrayed to the People's Government, charged with stealing from the orphanage. He was taken into custody and he was held in solitary for 8 months, brought out and tortured for 3 days and 4 nights, or perhaps it was 4 nights and 3 days, and by that time he was ready to confess anything. He made his confession and what it was he does not now remember. Bringing the account books to him, they asked him to show where he had taken this money, and he could not. The poor fellow could not because he had not stolen. They changed the charge to lying. He had lied to the People's Government. He had not taken the money, and he had confessed to taking it, and therefore they charged him with lying. So they tried him on that, and found him guilty and sentenced him to 3 years, and he served the 3 years at hard labor in a brickyard working with bare hands. He came out broken, of course, and was branded a criminal, so that he could not secure work, and he became a rice louse, begging from stoop to stoop.

After 18 months and after many trips to headquarters, he persuaded the authorities to allow him to get to Hong Kong. There is movement to and fro, as you know, across the border. Right now there are as many as 40,000 refugees fleeing from the marvelous liberties of communism in Red China to Hong Kong, where a desperate situation confronts them.

He got to Hong Kong, and he is now the treasurer of one of our largest orphanages, called the Peoples Garden. He had been there some 8 weeks when I came to see him. He had partially regained his strength but will never be the same. Death is marked on him.

When I got to Taipei, I told this experience to our Ambassador, Mr. Rankin, and he smiled and said, "Mr. Poling, that is it." He said, "To understand communism, you must understand why that could be. It is injustice, complete incredible disregard for the individual, but nevertheless it is the realism of communism."

He told me that in Nanking, shortly before the Embassy was moved, and while he was acting in the stead of Dr. Stuart who was then our Ambassador, but who was ill in the United States, there were two cases in one week in the People's Government court. In one a man was charged with the murder of his wife, and he was found guilty and sentenced to 90 days. In the other case, an employee of the People's Government was charged with stealing ink from the office. He was found guilty, sentenced to be executed, and his head was chopped off.

"Now," Mr. Rankin said, "there is just nothing in that that is understandable to a Christian, or to a free man anywhere in the world, is there? But to the Communists in the first instance the man had committed a purely personal crime; he murdered his own wife. He of course should be punished, and the criminal act should be recognized, but it was simply the murder of his wife. But in the second instance, the man had committed an offense against the People's Government. He had stolen ink from the People's Government. His offense was heinous, and it was complete, and he was sentenced to be executed and his head was chopped off."

Mr. ARENS. You have pointed out something that is almost incredible to the Western mind, and to a person who is inculcated with even the basic Christian precepts. Why is it, then, if communism is such a hideous force, that it has swept over vast areas of the earth with such incredible speed, and today threatens to engulf other areas of the earth?

Dr. POLING. How often I have asked myself that question. I found one answer. If you do not have anything—and this is the case in Asia particularly where millions of people wonder whether they may reasonably hope to have a handful of rice in the morning—a promise, even if it is a lie, is something. Now, that is one answer. That is part of the answer to the question. Communism purports to offer the answer to multitudes and millions of people, underprivileged, hungry, starving. Communism moves in on us at our weakest point. They blow up the great lie of colonialism and charges of imperialism. You know Goebbels said that if you repeat a lie often enough, people will believe it, and you will even come to believe it yourself.

Now, for instance, at the present time there is the great falsehood about our inciting armed conflict along the Syrian frontier. I don't believe that anyone at the beginning believed that. I cannot understand how anyone could. Of course, there are millions who have no background knowledge at all, and along comes this accusation. After what happened in Hungary, after communism has made, in the opinion of some of us, a moral debacle of the United Nations, here comes the statement, bald and bold, that we are instigating armed conflict on the Syrian frontier. Now, some people give a measure of truth to that. And against the incident at Suez, and against all that has happened in the past, bringing it forward, and holding it up in front of the people, you find multitudes and multitudes believing.

Also, communism moves in on the very humanities of our Christian leaders. We should be men of mercy. We should believe rather than doubt. It is so easy for us, many of us, to be betrayed. Again and again men in whom I have great confidence and for whom I hold great admiration have associated themselves in resolutions with groups that were set up to subvert, to distract, and to draw attention away from the central fact. They signed petitions and letters and resolutions. They are not doing as much of it now as they did formerly, because, here a little and there a little, we have been able to bring to their attention the fallacy and the fact that in the name of the highest and the holiest, these men are moving to destroy the very freedoms that make it possible for us to speak out.

You see, after all, freedom has not yet perfected its processes, but as I said to a friend in Calcutta 3 years ago, the genius and the greatness of American freedom is this: that we may march and that we may move in the direction of the ultimate. Granted that mistakes have been made, and granted that not all of freedoms guaranteed by the Constitution and the Bill of Rights have been achieved, nevertheless we are free to move toward perfect freedom. The goal is in front of us, and we are on the march. That is the difference today between America and Communist countries.

Mr. ARENS. Dr. Poling, how can the forces of freedom undertake to stem the tide of communism? Can we negotiate binding agreements with them?

Dr. POLING. Speaking to a small group at the Williams Club last week I said that there was every reason for us to withdraw recognition of Russia; every reason for us to go back to the nonrecognition policy fixed by Secretary of State Colby in his letter to President Wilson, which was a fixed policy of the United States Government for the remainder of the Wilson administration, going through Harding and Coolidge and Hoover. Every agreement entered into by the Communists has been violated and it is apparent they deliberately moved to deceive. Here they have become in the embassy, and in the consular offices, centers for espionage and for traitorous acts. Therefore, there is every reason for us to do that.

I also said that I believe that for us to withdraw recognition would strengthen our position internationally, and certainly it would strengthen our position in all free Asian lands.

But then, I added, if, with the greater wisdom of the Government and with the greater responsibility of the Government—and the Government is responsible—if it is now impossible to take this radical action, then for freedom's sake, and for God's sake against atheism, let us not act as though we believed the great lie.

In other words, let us not deceive ourselves, and let us not deceive our allies, and let us make it perfectly clear that while we are compelled to go on with these negotiations, nevertheless we do so with our eyes open and we do not believe the great lie.

Mr. ARENS. How can the free world contain communism, which is moving apparently with a relentless force over the world?

Dr. POLING. I believe that so-called peaceful coexistence is both incredible and impossible. As far as communism is concerned, so far as the Kremlin is concerned, it means to them peaceful submission. That is what it means. We need to face that fact. We must realize that. Whatever we do, we must act accordingly. Peaceful coexistence to the Kremlin means peaceful submission. That is the result inevitably and finally.

Colonel HEIMLICH. Can we as Christians apply moral or other force against this movement, against this insatiable demand for more people and more space in the world?

Dr. POLING. I don't believe I quite got your question. I am not sure that I do.

Colonel HEIMLICH. Communism represents a force of evil, whereas we believe Christianity represents a force of good and all that is progress in the world.

Dr. POLING. That is right; communism is satanic.

Colonel HEIMLICH. How do we as Christians move against it?

Dr. POLING. I think every declaration pointing out the nature and effect of communism, made in the United Nations is to the good, and let us keep on making declarations, and let us not lose a single opportunity in spite of the fact that they are ignored and repudiated and cynically regarded. It is tragic, to say the least, but surely there are ways in which we can activate the resolution.

For instance, now we have named a man to go to Hungary. Hungary declines to receive him. We ought to act on that. We ought to say something about that, but nothing has been said yet. Perhaps something will be said. We should insist that that man go in.

I was in Germany in August, and I met a convention of over 7,000 young Germans. One hundred and eleven came from behind the Iron Curtain. A young Lutheran churchman said, "What happened in Hungary is ready to happen in Czechoslovakia, in Poland, and among the pitiful remnants of the Baltic countries. What happened in Hungary is ready to happen in Mother Russia herself. But," he said, "the tragedy from the standpoint of those of us who do not consent was this: When Hungary arose, there was no support."

"Now," he said, "certainly we were left under the impression that such action as that which occurred in Hungary was desired by the

West. Certainly it was promoted by the West, by the broadcasts, the Voice of America, and the rest, and yet nothing happened." He said, "We are not inclined to criticize; we don't know; but if something could have happened, if there could have been a quick declaration of moral support, staccato, just like that, we would have been encouraged. In the end there will be risings. This thing cannot be contained."

In other words, he believes, as I do, that communism has at its heart the seed of its own death, but it takes time for the seed to germinate, and it takes time for the seed to come to its harvest. All that we are doing now, with our preparedness—and whatever the cost that preparedness must not be skimped—all that we are doing is buying time, as I see it.

Mr. ARENS. What can the average Mr. and Mrs. American do, if anything, on behalf of the forces of freedom to stem the tide of communism at home and abroad?

Dr. POLING. There are several things we can do. We can first of all associate ourselves with those movements that are anti-Communist, definitely anti-Communist. For instance, there is the All American Conference to Combat Communism, which brings together officially representatives of more than 50 national organizations. These organizations have more than 60 million members. They are such organizations as the General Federation of Women's Clubs, and all of the veterans organizations that are nationally congressionally chartered, and their auxiliaries, such as the American Legion, Veterans of Foreign Wars, the Catholic War Veterans, and Jewish War Veterans, and all of the fraternal organizations that are nationally chartered, all of them, including such youth organizations as the International Society of Christian Endeavor, and Allied Youth.

More than that, I think that letterwriting where it is done intelligently and in good faith is helpful. I have, for example, written a letter to the New York Times, associating myself with that distinguished churchman, Bishop Welch, the senior bishop in the Methodist Church. We need to do more of that. We need to give support to the men out in front.

Herbert Philbrick is doing a fine thing in the Herald Tribune. There are many ways in which even the little man, the little woman, and the little person may get into this conflict and be identified with this movement. Above all, the individual citizen should support our own Christian patriotic organizations and institutions.

Then I think that I might well say that you gentlemen who are here today from the Committee on Un-American Activities of the House of Representatives represent the spearhead of the aggressive continuous attack on communism. I don't know what I would do without the material that comes month after month, and regularly, from Washington, D. C., and from your headquarters, because that is authoritative, and I use it in my column, "Americans All."

The very fact you and the committee are under attack is significant. If you were not doing something, you would not be under attack. You are out in front, as I say again; you are the spearhead of this attack. Your work is authoritative; it is official; and I am for it. I think that I would like to express my personal appreciation for it.

There is the work that J. Edgar Hoover does and the FBI, the constant and unfaltering work. I find that all over the United States

Mr. Hoover himself is regarded as one of the preeminent Americans whose integrity, whose patriotism, and whose intelligence and courage are not to be questioned.

Mr. ARENS. Do you have any thoughts which you would care to express, Dr. Poling, with reference to how the average American can detect within his own community, and within the orbit of his own activities, Communist infiltration and influence?

Dr. POLING. It is very difficult, and there the danger comes. I think it is so dangerous for us to name names, and to say, "This man is a Communist" or "This man is a subversive." But, nevertheless, we need to be alert to the fact that when it comes to basic American institutions and American freedoms, the man who is soft in his attitude toward these things, even though he may not be a subversive, is not a helpful fighter for freedom in our time. Those who come into print and associate themselves in the daily press with movements that have been, to say the least, far left of center, need to be answered, and we may answer them without indicting them, without questioning their integrity, and without questioning their basic loyalty.

You see, here it is: The man who is not a Communist—a card-bearing Communist—but who associates himself with such activities as many of my brother clergymen, too many of them, associated themselves with in the past, is worth more to communism than 100 card-bearing Communists, vastly more.

Mr. ARENS. How does the patriotic American of good intentions peer behind the appealing facade which the Communist operation puts up in this country for its various movements?

Dr. POLING. Can I tell you what my experience was? I wrote an article in the Saturday Evening Post 3 years ago to which they gave the title, "Preachers Are Citizens, Too." In it I spoke of three instances in which I had unwittingly identified myself with movements that in themselves I judged to be correct, but in which I was associated with men and women whom I did not wish to be associated with. I was lined up on the wrong side. So I reached the conclusion that I would sign no resolution that I did not write myself, or for which I was not fully responsible as to my knowledge of it. That came out of an experience with the distinguished president of a theological seminary who signed the petition which was sent to the President in support of clemency for the 11 convicted Communists. He signed it, and he was asked to sign it by a clergyman who lives in Philadelphia, who has organized such movements frequently. Eight months later when it was released he discovered that it was not what he had signed, and also that he was associated with those he did not wish to be associated with. He telephoned me here at this office for my advice, and I said, "Send a telegram to the President and also send a telegram to the gentleman in Philadelphia, in which you ask that your name be withdrawn, in which you state the case that this is not what you signed, and that you do not wish to be associated with those who are on that resolution or petition."

Then he wrote me a letter and he said, "What are we going to do?" I wrote an editorial in which I stated what I have just said to you: That I sign no resolutions that I do not write myself, or that I am not fully acquainted with as to their beginnings, as to their purpose, and, above all, as to those who are actually responsible for them.

Now, I think that that is the only safe course, and a multitude of men who previously were careless—and women, too—are not careless any longer, and we are not having as much difficulty as we used to have.

But on the other hand, it is not enough to be negative. We ought to be out in front with our proposals. For instance, there is this full-page advertisement in the New York Times by the Committee of One Million, in which the speech of Hu Shih, the distinguished Chinese, before the United Nations is given a full spread, in which he tells the awful story of communism in action on the mainland of China.

Mr. ARENS. Now, may I ask you finally, if you please, Dr. Poling, how can the forces of freedom best compete in the world market place of ideas with Communist ideology?

Dr. POLING. First of all, by being constructive. It is not enough to be negative. We must state the case for freedom and for democracy—what it has done.

For instance, when we are charged with colonialism, let us tell the story of the Philippine Islands. That was told so eloquently by Gen. Carlos Romulo, in which in 25 years, as of his statement, we accomplished more for the people of the Philippines, and now the Republic of the Philippines, than other great powers had accomplished in 100 years of colonializing in the Far East. We can tell that story of what we did, the millions we invested, in order that a people might be sanitary, that they might be educated, that they might be prepared for freedom. Then we gave them their freedom.

Now, you can see how it pays off, because we have no more loyal ally anywhere in the world than the Republic of the Philippines.

We need to tell the story of freedom—what it is. We made a mistake early in the days of our broadcasting of telling the world how wonderful we were, and what our economy was, and what our material living conditions were. I saw in one of the Indian English papers a cartoon. Uncle Sam was seated nonchalantly at the top of a pyramid of things—automobiles, deep freezes, and telephones—and nonchalantly smoking a cigar. At the base of this pyramid little people were staggering and falling and holding up their starved hands. That was presented as a picture of the United States of America.

A friend of mine whom I met first in the University of London said, "Now, Poling, that cartoon is a lie. I know that it is a lie." But nevertheless, that is released as a picture to these millions in India, and in Ceylon, and that is the story. He said, "For heaven's sake, go back and get the Voice of America to tell us something else, because we never expect to have deep freezes and bathtubs and automobiles."

But I repeat what I said before. They would like to know they may have a handful of rice in the morning. We have changed the Voice of America at that point. We need to emphasize not what material things we have here, but the realities of freedom and the fact that communism is slavery. It is the destruction of the very aspirations of the soul. It is enslavement of the body, and you can prove that by pointing to Communist slave camps all over the world; and not only the enslavement of the body, but the enslavement of the mind and the soul. And remember one thing: there are more than one billion human beings who believe in one God—the Moslem, the Buddhist, the Roman Catholic, the Protestant, and the Jew.

We should lay emphasis upon the fact that communism in its first tenet is atheism. We have obscured that idea too often. We need to point to what we have on our coins, "In God We Trust." We need to get that across, if you please. We are getting the dollar across, but we need to get across the thing that we really finally live by in this country.

Mr. ARENS. How do we point out the wolf of communism that is in sheep's clothing, which it presents to the peoples of the world?

Dr. POLING. By telling what it has done and how it was done, the rape of the Baltic countries, taking up those populations and throwing them out of their homes and lands and farms into Siberia; what it has meant in the slave camps; what it has meant in China, the admissions of Chou En-lai, where he admits to 800,000 human souls liquidated. I prefer to take the figures of Bishop Quinton Y. K. Wong, a bishop of the Episcopal Church in China, who finally escaped, and he is now in the Diocese of Pittsburgh. His estimate is that 40 million people were liquidated. We need to tell the true story and we need to make it graphic. We have been sometimes restrained by our own readers who have been timorous about exciting or disturbing relationships in the United Nations. Well, as I see it, more and more we need to be doing what we are doing now there, telling the truth, and just the truth about communism as it is. We can point out the sham of the promise of communism by showing its morbid, bloody results.

Mr. ARENS. Now, Dr. Poling, we have asked you a number of questions on each of several facets of this tremendous problem. Are there other areas that you would like to comment on, or anything else you have in mind which you would like to say?

Dr. POLING. Well, it is the human interest thing that holds me in a poignant grip. I have been going out and seeing these babies and children ever since 1946, in the Middle East, and then with the coming of the Korean war in 1950, in the Far East. They are children that I have come to love, and they are beautiful children. Here, for example [indicating], are some pictures that reached me today. Here is a picture of a little girl that Mrs. Poling made her very own. Oriental children are beautiful youngsters. This child saw her father beheaded. He was the head man of a small city 40 miles from Canton. She also saw two uncles beheaded, and she saw her family wiped out. Six years ago she was a little girl 7 years old, who fled screaming into the night. How she ever got across, I don't know, but she is now in our orphanage. We call it the Faith Love Orphanage in Hong Kong.

Mr. ARENS. What denomination, may I ask?

Dr. POLING. It is interdenominational. The Christian Herald is nondenominational. When I first saw this child, she could not smile. As you see from these pictures, she smiles all over now. These other pictures are of children that were starved. Do you know that 6 years ago when we took the census in our Faith Love Orphanage, 80.7 percent of those children were children of fathers who had been liquidated? The clearer word for that is murdered by Communists when they came into south China.

Now, don't ask me to be too calm about this thing. Don't suggest to me peaceful coexistence for this thing. If I believe—and I do believe in the Christian ethic—if I believe in the words of Jesus, who said, "Suffer the little children to come unto me and forbid them not," if these things are real to me, then communism which is anti-God, is forever and eternally my enemy.

Mr. ARENS. It has been suggested, if I could interpose this comment just so our record is clear, that communism is after all only an economic system. I believe it was the present leader of the Kremlin, Khrushchev, who speaks of two competing economic systems. Do you have an observation to make on that?

Dr. POLING. It is very simple. That, of course, is part of the great lie. Communism is a total and comprehensive philosophy. It is a way of life. It is a coverall, body, mind, and soul. It is the universal enslavement.

Mr. ARENS. Thank you, Dr. Poling, for your contribution in this consultation on "The Ideological Fallacies of Communism."

(Thereupon, at 3:20 p. m., Friday, October 18, 1957, the staff consultation was concluded.)

INDEX

INDIVIDUALS

www.ingramcontent.com/pod-product-compliance
Lightning Source LLC
Chambersburg PA
CBHW081540280526
45788CB00010B/3302